Stoic Entrepreneurship

Embracing Challenges and Building Success

Table of Contents

Chapter 1. Introduction

Discover the unfathomable power of Stoic Entrepreneurship in our latest Special Report - "Stoic Entrepreneurship: Embracing Challenges and Building Success." This intriguing discourse peels back the layers of ancient Stoic philosophy, seamlessly blending it with the audacious spirit of contemporary entrepreneurship. Grapple with your business challenges like never before, guided by a fusion of timeless wisdom and modern tactics, crafted to ensure resilience and prosperity. Our special report is a vibrant beacon, shining new light on entrepreneurship, motivating the aspirant in you to boldly confront obstacles and harness them into stepping stones for success. This isn't a mere assimilation of ideas; it's a rejuvenating journey that embarks you on the path of triumphant entrepreneurship. Get ready for a deep voyage within, powering through uncertainties, and emerging with an entrepreneurial mindset honed by stoic tenacity. Buckle up, for this is the most stimulating investment you'll make for your entrepreneurial journey!

Chapter 2. Unveiling Stoic Philosophy

Before diving into an in-depth exploration of the Stoic philosophy and how it pertains to entrepreneurial ventures, let's embark on a brief trip through the annals of history for better context.

It is to the Hellenistic period in Athens around 300 BC that we owe the conception of Stoicism. Stoicism was founded by Zeno of Citium but notably, its teachings were further carried forward by the likes of Epictetus, Seneca, and Marcus Aurelius. Like other philosophical doctrines, it sought to answer the profound inquiries of life and existence but what set Stoicism apart was its practical approach to the trials and tribulations of everyday life.

2.1. The Four Pillars of Stoicism

Stoicism as a philosophy is fundamentally built upon four virtues — Wisdom, Courage, Justice, and Temperance.

Wisdom, in the Stoic sense, goes beyond mere academic knowledge. It represents a profound understanding of nature, consciousness and the cosmos. It is the basis through which one can discern right from wrong and circumstances as indifferent.

Courage within Stoicism refers not only to physical courage but also to moral courage. It is the will to stand for what is right, irrespective of the discomfort it causes. It is the resilience to endure suffering, a virtue of paramount importance for any entrepreneur.

Justice, to the Stoics, is the cornerstone of social harmony. It dictates fair dealings not grounded merely upon self-interest but also on societal welfare. As an entrepreneur, acknowledging justice means ensuring fair practices within your establishment and towards your clientele.

Temperance, lastly, is the practice of self-restraint and moderation. It preaches avoiding excess and indulgences. For the stoic entrepreneur, temperance is avoiding the glamour and allurements that come with success, it is resisting the urge to prioritize profits over people or process.

2.2. Taking Comfort in Indifference

The principle of indifference stands at the crux of Stoic teachings. The Stoic worldview categorizes events as either within our control or outside of it. By taking comfort in indifference towards uncontrollable events, the Stoic entrepreneur places his focus squarely on what he can influence, leading to clearer decision-making and stress mitigation.

With constant evolution and change being the only constants in a business environment, this tenet becomes paramount, encouraging entrepreneurs to stay grounded and focus on areas within their sphere of influence.

2.3. Coping with Negative Emotions

Stoicism gives a new perspective on how to manage plagued emotions like anger, anxiety, disappointment, and despair. For Stoics, experiencing negative emotions means failing to comprehend the nature of things.

When translated into a business context, the outcome of an investor meeting, response to a new product launch, or effects of market changes are seen as indifferent. They are externalities which should not govern your inner peace. Instead, they should be used as resources to learn and adapt, further preparing your venture for future challenges.

2.4. Embracing the Dichotomy of Control

Entrepreneurs who imbibe Stoicism are urged to adopt the Stoic belief of Dichotomy of Control - acknowledging the influence of external factors on outcomes while maintaining utmost dedication to internal efforts.

Instead of infuriating over a declined deal, you focus on iterating your proposal. Rather than brooding over a failed campaign, you analyze the reasons and plan for a better one. This balance, this dichotomy of control, allows for an environment for learning and constant progression, rather than destructive dejection or unhelpful elation.

These apparitions of Stoic philosophy lay the foundation for Stoic Entrepreneurship, a harmony of ancient wisdom, and modern entrepreneurial spirit. Armed with resilience, individuals engaged in this philosophy can turn the incubus of failure into a phantasm of fortitude, propelling towards not just success, but a content, fulfilled entrepreneurial journey. A venture where temporal setbacks do not decrease morale, where success does not lead to complacency, essentially creating a center from where the entrepreneur, much like the stoic, can endure the highs and lows with an equanimous temperament.

2.5. All is Perspective

"Life is not the way it's supposed to be, it's the way it is. The way you cope with it is what makes the difference" - Virginia Satir.

Stoicism and entrepreneurship share a fundamental attribute - perspective. Successful entrepreneurs, like good Stoics, are able to decipher between the realities of the world and their perceptions. A failed product is not a sign to capitulate but a signal to pivot.

Criticisms aren't personal attacks, but instrumental resources for betterment.

While embracing Stoic values won't ensure the absence of adversity, it certainly equips one with the mental fortitude to navigate through the maelstrom that the entrepreneurial whelm is. It offers a purpose-driven approach to entrepreneurship, grounded in a robust understanding of oneself and the cosmos, guided by a moral compass, fortified by resilience, and predicated on the acceptance of inevitable challenges.

As we venture further into the realms of stoic entrepreneurship, we understand that stoicism isn't a philosophy for the weak but a mantra for the willing - willing to adapt, persevere and ultimately win. It isn't for those who wish to stagnate but those who strive to ascend. Like the phoenix that rises from the ashes, a stoic entrepreneur views failure not as a rueful end but as a rejuvenating beginning, a commencement of another stride towards success.

We now approach the next chapter equipped with a foundational understanding of Stoic philosophy, ready to delve deeper into the application of these principles within the business world.

Chapter 3. Lessons from the Stoics: Embracing Adversities

The power of Stoicism, as conceived by the ancient philosophers, lies not in its ability to simply transcend adversities, but to utilize them as integral components of personal and professional growth. Stoicism, therefore embodies the concept, "what doesn't kill you, makes you stronger." For the stoic entrepreneur, adversity isn't an obstruction, it's a whetstone against which they sharpen their entrepreneurial acumen.

3.1. Using Adversity as a Tool

Instead of being an obstacle on the path to success, the stoic entrepreneur views adversity as a tool that can be used to sculpt their character and refine their actions. Such a perspective offers three key advantages:

1. It fundamentally alters our approach to adversity by transforming it from an enemy to be feared into a companion to be embraced.

2. It transforms adversity from an inhibitor of progress to a catalyst for growth.

3. It allows us to channel adversity in a constructive way, retracing it from the path of destruction to the path of construction.

This mental reframing of adversity enables us to venture forth fearlessly into the unknown, confronting and transforming challenges into milestones on our journey to success.

3.2. Adversity as a Guide

The ancient stoic philosophers like Seneca, Epictetus and Marcus Aurelius believed that adversity carries with it a powerful message. It's a call to action, a call to rethink our strategies, evaluate our strengths, recognize our weaknesses and surmount our limitations. By actively tracing the messages hidden within adversities, we can devise plans that help us surmount them, while strengthening our resilience and improving our strategic thinking.

3.3. Cultivating Resilience through Adversity

It's worth noting that resilience isn't an inherent trait, but one that can be cultivated over time. Stoic philosophy emphasizes the cultivation of resilience through continuous exposure to adversity. It suggests that intentional hardship, such as voluntarily subjecting oneself to difficult conditions or circumstances, or continuously pushing oneself to do more and achieve more, can foster resilience.

The stoic entrepreneurs, hence, intentionally create testing conditions that push their boundaries, enabling them to grow stronger in the face of adversity. This practice effectively fosters resilience and enhances the ability to power through difficulties, thus serving as a precursor to entrepreneurial success.

3.4. Lessons from Stoic Examples

Studying the real-life application of Stoic principles can produce a significant impact. One such example is the life of Elon Musk. Despite multiple failed launches and near bankruptcy, he maintained his stoic resolve, using adversity not as a reason to give up, but as a push to innovate, adapt, and overcome. Today, his companies are making revolutionary changes in various fields from space to renewable energy.

3.5. Thriving under Pressure

Instead of succumbing to pressure, the Stoic entrepreneur learns to thrive under it. Pressure is perceived not as a hindrance, but as an opportunity to rise to the occasion. Considering high-stakes situations as a chance to excel rather than an impasse can effectively enable the diversion of pressure from a heat source to a power source.

3.6. Overcoming Fear with Action

Fear is often a significant factor that limits our ability to act. Stoic philosophy teaches that fear can be overcome by taking focused actions towards our goals. By directing our energy towards action and solutions rather than on fear and problems, we can effectively navigate through adversities.

3.7. The Mindset Shift

This entire discourse boils down to shifting the mindset, a pivot of perspective regarding adversity's role in our entrepreneurial journey. By becoming a stoic entrepreneur, we agree to use adversity to our advantage, to serve as our tool, guide, and medium to build resilience, making adversity our comrade rather than an adversary. This mindset shift ushered by stoic philosophy becomes the cornerstone of successful, unstoppable entrepreneurship.

In conclusion, embracing adversity is a skill that can be honed and utilized in the entrepreneurial landscape. Adversity, reframed through the lens of Stoicism, can provide invaluable guidance in strategy, push limits to foster resilience, inspire action overcoming fear, and ultimately, yield an empowering mindset shift, catapulting the stoic entrepreneur in the direction of success.

Chapter 4. Modern Entrepreneurship: An Ocean of Challenges

In an era as dynamic as the one we live in today, entrepreneurship is nothing short of an unending expedition. With its labyrinthine turns, it mirrors an ocean, vast and unfathomable, filled with unimaginable challenges and unpredictable opportunities. While the currents of this ocean are perpetually changing, the spirit of the entrepreneur, built on resilience and endurance, stands unwavering.

4.1. Entering the Waters: The Start of the Journey

The entrepreneurial journey begins with an idea, a spark, something that catches your mind's eye and refuses to let go. It is here that you step into the waters of entrepreneurship. This is an exhilarating time full of potential and possibility, but it is also fraught with challenges. Capital investment, building a dedicated team, market evaluation, and creating a scalable business model are among the daunting tasks that you face. The unfathomable power of Stoic philosophy can assist entrepreneurship in taking these challenges in stride. As Marcus Aurelius, Roman Emperor and a prominent stoic philosopher, stated, "The impediment to action advances action. What stands in the way becomes the way."

4.2. Navigating the High Seas: Stepping into the Market

Stepping into the market is like navigating the high seas. A potent mix of competition, customer acquisition, and consistent value delivery make the waters choppy and tempestuous. The winds of market change are rapid and at times brutal; understanding and accommodating for these changes is not just important, it's essential for survival. At this junction, entrepreneurship needs to be armed with the stoic principle of detachment from external circumstances and absolute control over one's reaction to them.

Understand, stoicism does not propose inaction; rather, it advises a measured response, free from the propensity of being 'swept away' by the situation. Stoics regard difficulties as teachers and shape them into stepping stones for success. They recognize their own role in shaping their perception of reality, ensuring that their view of the situation remains untainted by emotion or prejudice.

4.3. Storms and Calms: Dealing with Uncertainties and Volatility

Expecting calm waters throughout your entrepreneurial journey would be tantamount to wishful thinking. The ocean of entrepreneurship is laden with storms of uncertainty, unpredictability, and volatility. It is in such tempests that many shipwreck, succumbing to the pressure and unpredictability of business storms. Yet, it is also in these testing times that the essence of stoic philosophy shines brightest.

Stoic philosophy emphasizes embracing uncertainty, viewing it as part of life's experiences rather than a malaise to be eradicated. It teaches us to differentiate between what we can control and what we cannot, enabling us to focus our energy on what's within our sphere of influence. This principle of stoicism provides a solid framework within which entrepreneurs can withstand business storms and emerge stronger, with enriched insights and sturdier resilience.

4.4. Endless Horizon: The Aspect of Constant Growth

The ceaseless ocean of entrepreneurship stretches out towards an endless horizon. The aspect of constant growth is inherent in its vast expanse. However, with growth come bigger challenges, larger responsibilities, and a sterner test of endurance. A growing business reflects a growing number of stakeholders and an expansive network of operations – all of which may seem overwhelming.

Here is where another Stoic principle comes into play – the principle of 'Amor Fati' or 'love of fate.' It is about not just simply accepting, but dearly embracing the events that life throws at us, good or bad. This belief cultivates an attitude of enthusiastically welcoming growth and its accompanying challenges, converting potential anxieties into anticipation.

4.5. The Voyage Within: Cultivating the Entrepreneurial Mindset

The active navigation through the complex ocean of entrepreneurship is not just about external management; it includes a deep voyage within. Cultivating an entrepreneurial mindset is about developing the fortitude to withstand hardships, the foresight to seize opportunities, the tenacity to persist in the face of failure, and the humility to learn from every experience.

Stoic philosophy, with its stress on presence of mind, emotional intelligence, and growth from adversity, is a potent tool for cultivating this mindset. It challenges us to confront our deepest fears, urging us to harness them as catalysts for growth and transformation. This voyage within paves the path for entrepreneurial success, moulded by the unfathomable power of stoic tenacity.

In conclusion, entrepreneurship, like the ocean, is a vast, unending entity, full of formidable challenges and untapped opportunities. Yet, just as the ocean is a source of life, entrepreneurship is a source of opportunities. By harnessing potent ideas tucked within the philosophy of stoicism, the entrepreneurial expedition through this ocean can transform from a perilous journey into an enlightening voyage, a journey that doesn't just aim at success, but at an inspired, resilient, and enlightened life. As Seneca, the Stoic philosopher, aptly said, "A gem cannot be polished without friction, nor a man perfected without trials."

Chapter 5. Stoic Entrepreneurship: The Intersection of Antiquity and Modernity

The dynamic transformation of the economic landscape has bred a new breed of entrepreneurs - a fusion of old and new, the 'Stoic Entrepreneur.'

5.1. The Roots of Stoicism

The seed of Stoicism was sown in the rich soil of ancient Greece, where it blossomed into a profound philosophical system. Its core tenets urge us to master our perceptions and emotions, to discern between what we can and cannot change, and to bravely face life with equanimity. These principles gifted the ancient Greeks with serenity and resilience amidst life's tempests. Today, we can harness these age-old teachings to fortify ourselves against the tumultuous challenges of entrepreneurship.

5.2. Embracing Stoicism in the Modern Business Landscape

Nicholas Nassim Taleb, the acclaimed author of "The Black Swan," encapsulates the essence of the Stoic entrepreneur: "A Stoic is a Buddhist with an attitude." This attitude, one of resilience and resolve, adds an extraordinary layer to the entrepreneurial journey, empowering one to navigate the ups and downs of business with unwavering grit.

Stoicism encourages us to acknowledge our fears, hold them beneath the magnifying glass of introspection, and extract valuable lessons from them. A Stoic entrepreneur embraces challenges, associates them not with dread but opportunities for growth and triumph. Amidst uncertainty, they find solidity; in adversity, they see a chance for evolution.

5.3. Instilling Stoic Resilience

How do we plant Stoic resilience into the core of our entrepreneurial spirits? This is no light task; it necessitates a paradigm shift. Entrepreneurs normally view business issues solely in a contemporary context, often overlooking the Universal Laws that govern our existence. Stoic philosophy urges us to recognize these Immutable Laws, such as the Law of Change, the Law of Cause & Effect, and the Law of Polarity. Realizing that change is inevitable, that every action has an equal and opposite reaction, that everything has an opposite, enables entrepreneurs to see setbacks in a new, empowering light.

The ability to sustain a bird-eye view, to behold every business challenge within the larger tapestry of Universal Laws, breeds unshakeable resilience. An entrepreneur who grasps this transcends the narrow perception of failure as a 'setback' and sees it as a stepping stone, an intrinsic part of the grand dance of entrepreneurial success.

5.4. The Stoic Entrepreneur's Toolkit

Phenomenal is the transformative power of Stoic tenets when wielded skilfully in the domain of entrepreneurship. Here, we dissect the key attributes worn by the Stoic entrepreneur:

- Stoic Vision: Stoic entrepreneurs approach their enterprise with a grand vision. They comprehend the Law of Cause & Effect, mindful that each decision shapes the trajectory of their venture. Stoic vision guards against shortsightedness, nurturing long-term thinking and strategic action.

- Stoic Courage: Stoicism never promises a life devoid of tribulations; instead, it trains us to face adversity head-on, fuelled by courage and resilience.

- Stoic Acceptance: This is crucial for entrepreneurs who teeter on the precipice of uncertainty. Stoic entrepreneurs celebrate the ebb and flow of business, understanding the duality of success and failure.

- Stoic Wisdom: Stoic entrepreneurs don't merely acquire knowledge - they cultivate wisdom. They embed themselves in continuous learning, always acquiring and applying knowledge to the ever-evolving business environment.

5.5. A New Dawn in Entrepreneurship

As the realms of ancient wisdom and modern entrepreneurship collide, a new era in business is ushered in - the era of the Stoic Entrepreneur. By harnessing the power of Stoic philosophy, today's entrepreneurs can weather the most turbulent business storms, turning the stumbling blocks of entrepreneurship into stepping stones towards success. The intersection of antiquity and modernity fosters an entrepreneurial mindset that skilfully navigates the ebbs and flows of the business world, paving the way for a future teeming with prosperity, resilience, and enduring success.

Stoic Entrepreneurship is not a mere combination of two disparate worlds, but a bold evolution in thinking and doing. It's a creative dance between wisdom and action, between reflection and execution. It stands as a reminder that in the face of incessant change, timeless principles remain our guiding beacon. Thus, in the heart of stoic entrepreneurship lies the paradox of constancy amidst change, of calm amidst chaos, and success amidst struggles. Welcome to a brave new world where the past and the present no longer clash, but merge... in the audacious journey of the Stoic Entrepreneur.

Chapter 6. Resilience Matters: Stoic Strategies for Entrepreneurs

The entrepreneurial journey is one of tempestuous trials and tribulations. It's an uncharted path filled with precipitous peaks and dappled with daunting valleys. There are triumphant times of scaling new heights, but equally, if not more oftentimes, entrepreneurship demands one to face failure, confront uncertainty, and grapple with challenges that seemingly have insurmountable odds.

The art of cultivating resilience, an essence of Stoic philosophy, is an infallible asset for entrepreneurs, empowering them to endure these trials, adapt to changes, and thrive amidst adversity. By internalizing Stoic principles, entrepreneurs can exercise resilience to transform obstacles into opportunities, challenges into catalysts, and setbacks into comebacks.

6.1. Stoicism: The Primer

Stoicism, a philosophy conceived by ancient Greeks, places emphasis on virtue, temperance, and wisdom. It encourages understanding things as they are, not as we wish them to be. At its core, Stoicism is about recognizing what we can control and accepting what we cannot, distinguishing between ephemeral disturbances and lasting happiness, and appreciating the present moment.

For entrepreneurs, recognizing this power of control equates to acknowledging the difference between external business circumstances and their internal reactions. It's about understanding that success isn't defined by outward measures alone, but also by the stalwart strength and tenacity possessed internally.

6.2. Cultivating Emotional Resilience

Stoics venerated emotional resilience, a trait that bestows individuals with the determination and courage to persistently overcome adversity. The essence of Stoic philosophy encourages us to not just experience emotions, but to understand, analyze, and desensitize our responses to them. The understanding of our emotional selves is a superweapon towards cultivation of resilience in entrepreneurship.

A stoic entrepreneur exercises emotional intelligence, controlling his/her reactions rather than being controlled by them. This implies discerning the difference between failing at a task and being a failure, between a temporary setback and a permanent end. Such entrepreneurs believe in the potential of bouncing back, equipped with the lessons from these same setbacks, turning them into forceful steps towards success.

6.3. Embracing Change: The Stoic Way

Change is a relentless constant in both life and business, and entrepreneurs are required to adeptly navigate this ever-changing landscape. The ability to embrace and adapt to change, while maintaining a firm resolve, is a chief tenet of Stoic philosophy, and of entrepreneurial resilience.

A Stoic entrepreneur proactively adopts change, even chaos, not as an intrusive threat but as a vista of opportunities. Instead of resisting, they acclimate, thus transforming unexpected scenarios into profitable prospects, and riding the waves of change rather than being swept by them.

6.4. The Indomitable Power of Perspective

Perspective, the linchpin of Stoic philosophy, allows one to perceive the same situation differently. For the resilient stoic-minded entrepreneur, a challenge is not a stumbling block but a stepping-stone, every failure a lesson, and every criticism a chance for refinement.

Endowed with an adaptive and optimistic perspective, such an entrepreneur turns adversity into advantage, refashions disappointment into determination, and converts improbable challenges to probable triumphs. This mental robustness stems from the perpetual ability to shift perspective and look beyond the immediate discomfort to the ultimate growth derived from it.

6.5. Navigating Uncertainty: The Stoic Approach

Uncertainty is a near-permanent resident in an entrepreneur's life. The Stoics proposed dealing with it by focusing on resilient attitudes and proactive strategies rather than fearing it.

The stoic entrepreneur revels in uncertainty, viewing it as a test of their entrepreneurial mettle. Instead of allowing fear of the unknown to hinder their progress, they adopt a proactive stance, seeking solutions and developing strategies to rise above the fog of uncertainty. They embrace the fact that outside conditions will never be perfect, but it is the inner stability that makes the difference.

6.6. Building Stoic Habits for Resilient Entrepreneurship

Practicing stoicism is not a one-off act but rather a continuous exercise in self-awareness, discipline, and reflection. Cultivating stoic habits equates to creating a buffer of emotional, psychological, and intellectual strength that transforms one's approach to challenging situations.

As an entrepreneur, incorporating daily rituals of Stoic readings, meditation, journaling self-reflections, constant learning, regular re-evaluations, proactive adjustments, and cultivating gratitude can significantly foster resilience. These habits allow them to anticipate, prepare for, and thrive amidst trials, thereby embodying true stoic entrepreneurship.

In essence, stoic entrepreneurship is about developing a resilient mindset that sees challenges not as debilitating dead-ends but as invigorating detours paving the way for success. By studying and imitating the Stoics' emotional resilience, acceptance of change, positive perspectives, uncertainty navigation strategies, and their daily habits, entrepreneurs can enhance their resilience, making them unstoppable in the face of any adversity. This path, while arduous, ultimately leads to a robust, resilient, and rewarding entrepreneurial journey. The furrows of failures and meandering paths of challenges converge to form the straight road to success for the true Stoic entrepreneur.

Chapter 7. Harnessing Challenges: From Obstacles to Opportunities

There's a grit to entrepreneurship that demands a certain resolve; a robustness that enables one to grapple with uncertainty and challenges — and emerge triumphant. To nurture this intrinsic quality, we look towards the Stoic philosophy, smelting the strength within you to turn obstacles into opportunities.

7.1. The Stoic Perspective on Challenges

Stoicism, an ancient Greek philosophy, pivots on the perception of control. Epictetus, a revered Stoic philosopher, articulated this principle: "We should always be asking ourselves: 'Is this something that is, or is not, in my control?'" This Stoic aphorism serves as a compass, helping us discern certain elements within our control — our actions, decisions, and attitudes — from uncontrollable external circumstances.

In entrepreneurship, our journey parallels this challenging course. Ramifications abound within the entrepreneurial landscape — fluctuations in market forces, aggressive competition, shifting consumer behavior — are inevitable constituents of running a business. Dovetailing Stoic philosophy into entrepreneurial practices, we seek to govern our reactions to these circumstances, mastering the art of converting impediments into launching pads for success.

Exploring this path, we need to reassess the way we perceive challenges, not as boulders blocking our path but as stepping stones, chiseling our entrepreneurial journey.

7.2. Transforming Challenges into Opportunities

Much of transforming challenges into opportunities is a result of an attitudinal shift. The goal is not to eliminate the challenge — the goal is to eliminate the negativity associated with it. Stoics believe that inherent negativity does not exist; it is our perception that paints situations as 'negative.' Here, we are reminded of another tenet of Stoic philosophy, from Marcus Aurelius: "The obstacle on the path becomes the way."

To an entrepreneur with a Stoic mindset, a challenge is merely a circumstance devoid of emotional attachment. It stands as a proposition, a riddle that needs to be unraveled, rather than a hurdle to be feared. This pivotal shift in perception reframes defeat as temporary, adversity as a learning opportunity, and struggles as necessary routes towards growth.

7.3. Implementing a Stoic Strategy: RESPOND

As entrepreneurs, the challenges we encounter are diverse and multifaceted, demanding a systematic and holistic responding strategy. Stoicism offers a solution - the RESPOND framework.

Strategy	Description
Rationalization	Assess the situation objectively, understanding its scope and impact on your enterprise objectively.

Strategy	Description
Emotional Distance	Maintain emotional neutrality towards the situation, fostering clear and logical decision-making.
Solution Originating	Identify the opportunity hidden within the challenge, generating solutions that capitalize on it.
Perception Altering	Shift your perception of the challenge from negative to neutral, thereby reducing emotional strain.
Operationalizing Actions	Put your solutions into practice, transforming your decisions into tangible actions.
Nourishing Resilience	Use the situation as a catalyst for resilience, building capacity for future challenges.
Diligence	Persistently pursue your actions, maintaining a relentless focus on your entrepreneurial goals.

Navigating entrepreneurship via the RESPOND framework, you wield challenges as tools that sharpen your venture, molding it to withstand adversity. To delve deeper, let's scrutinize the individual components of the RESPOND framework.

7.4. A Closer View: Deciphering the RESPOND Strategy

7.4.1. R: Rationalization

In essence, Stoicism promotes the cogent assessment of reality. To exercise rationalization, assess the situation neutrally. What is the challenge? How does it affect your venture? This stoic inquiry disentangles thought from emotion, allowing us to truly understand the issue, free from emotional bias.

7.4.2. E: Emotional Distance

Maintaining emotional distance from challenges is fundamental in Stoic philosophy. This practice paves the way for clear-headed decision-making processes. As an entrepreneur, it's crucial to avoid letting emotions cloud your judgment, ensuring that your decision-making is data-driven and objective.

7.4.3. S: Solution Originating

As the rational and emotional groundwork has been laid, it's time to burgeon solutions. Instead of viewing the problem as an insurmountable wall, see it as an opportunity for innovation. Various exercises support this practice, including brainstorming, mind mapping, or utilizing design thinking strategies.

7.4.4. P: Perception Altering

Alter your perception of the challenge — rewrite the narrative. Is it an insurmountable obstacle or a stepping stone? Is it a setback or an opportunity to learn, adapt, and improve?

7.4.5. O: Operationalizing Actions

Once a solution has been sculpted, it's time to breathe life into it. Implement your strategies on the operational level. Be proactive and deliberate with your execution, ensuring that every decision and action aligns with your overall entrepreneurial vision.

7.4.6. N: Nourishing Resilience

Each challenge navigated embeds resilience into the roots of your enterprise. Like a pearl in an oyster, resilience is cultivated layer by layer. Every challenge you confront and problem you solve contributes to your resiliency deposits, fortifying your venture for future trials.

7.4.7. D: Diligence

Stoicism values persistence and grit. Incorporate diligence into your entrepreneurial ethos. Implementing solutions is only half the journey; sustaining and monitoring them requires perseverance.

7.5. Infusing Stoic Tenets into Entrepreneurship: A Symbiosis

Bringing Stoicism into entrepreneurship does not mean discarding any other strategies or methodologies you are following. It's about finding a symbiosis between this ancient philosophy and your existing modus operandi. The stoic entrepreneur sits at the intersection of the past and the future, drawing wisdom from ancient philosophy while shaping the technology-infused marketplace of today. By embedding stoic practices into our behavior, we arm ourselves with a mindset that doesn't shy away from challenges but welcomes them as opportunities for growth.

By embracing the tenets of Stoic philosophy, we equip ourselves with tools that reframe our perspective and reinforce our resilience. It pushes us to grow, innovate, and cultivate an entrepreneurial landscape that thrives in the face of adversity. With Stoicism as your guiding principle and the RESPOND strategy as your compass, convert obstacles into opportunities, riding the tumultuous waves of entrepreneurship to the shores of success.

Chapter 8. Stoicism in Practice: Case Studies of Stoic Entrepreneurs

Gain a deeper understanding of stoic entrepreneurship in action as we delve into real-world case studies that exhibit how these principles can transform business strategies, leadership style, and personal conduct.

8.1. The Cold Logic of Jeff Bezos

First off, let's examine mega mogul Jeff Bezos, who harnessed stoic principles to catapult Amazon.com from a simple online bookstore into a global conglomerate encompassing e-commerce, cloud computing, digital streaming, and artificial intelligence.

His practices are embedded with the essence of stoicism. Confronted with competitors, critics, and market volatility, Bezos consistently illustrated rational thought, emotional control, and acceptance of the uncontrollable. 'Our job is to not be surprised', he famously stated, emphasizing the poignant stoic strategy of anticipating setbacks and meeting them with a well-measured reaction.

Even during Amazon's early days, while critics predicted an imminent demise, he held firm, calling it 'Day 1.' This stoic philosophy of regarding every day as an opportunity to start anew, perpetually in a state of newness, and striving for improvement, underpinned the unfathomable growth that Amazon experienced.

8.2. Phil Knight's Resiliency

Next, we will look at Phil Knight, the co-founder of Nike. His memoir,

Shoe Dog, is a testament to a stoic approach in navigating the rugged terrain of entrepreneurship. Nike began as Blue Ribbon Sports, importing high-quality running shoes from Japan. Knight faced countless adversities - legal battles, cash flow issues, and relationship breakdowns.

Yet, imbued with a stoic resolve, he remained unphased. Knight took obstacles in stride and even said, 'Let everyone else call your idea crazy...just keep going', reflecting the stoic principle of maintaining focus on one's path regardless of external opinion. Undeterred setbacks became opportunities, and Knight's application of stoicism spurred Nike's evolution into a global sports icon.

8.3. The Patient Prowess of Warren Buffet

Warren Buffet, arguably one of the most successful investors of all time, embodies stoicism through his patient and long-term approach. Buffet's investment philosophy, firmly rooted in stoic ideals, shuns impulsive decisions and market hysteria, focusing instead on intrinsic value and timeless principles.

His famous quote, 'The stock market is a device to transfer money from the impatient to the patient', reinforces the stoic virtue of patience - viewing market volatility as external noise that should not disturb one's equanimity. This stoic stance has led him to accumulate unprecedented wealth and respect in the finance world over his long career.

8.4. Angela Ahrendts - Stoicism in Leadership

Drawing our attention to Angela Ahrendts, former CEO of Burberry and Senior Vice President of Apple, her leadership style is deeply influenced by stoicism. She believes in the power of soft values like trust, intuition, and empathy, drawing parallels with stoic principles.

Indeed, Ahrendts is known for turning Burberry around by not only enhancing their product line but also by forging a unified company culture that celebrates empathy - a distinctive trait of stoic philosophy.

Each of these cases brilliantly demonstrates the diverse application of stoicism in entrepreneurship, showing that it is more than just a philosophical theory. It empowers perceptive multitasking strategies, adaptability, and endurance in tumultuous situations. By imbuing stoic principles into their work ethic, these entrepreneurs have revolutionized their respective fields, emerging victorious against all odds, embodying a potent blend of stoic resilience and entrepreneurial spirit. Such wisdom is inherently adaptable and universally applicable across diverse domains of business, commerce, and life. This compilation of case studies serves as a launchpad, allowing each reader to rethink, recalibrate and refine their entrepreneurial strategies through the lens of stoic philosophy. The timeless principles of stoicism prove to be a powerful tool set for personal growth and business success, a winning combination worth nurturing.

Chapter 9. Developing a Stoic Mindset: Practical Tactics

Stoic entrepreneurship is an unorthodox but incredibly effective approach to business, a fusion of timeless wisdom and twenty-first-century tactics. The bedrock foundation of this powerful paradigm is developing a stoic mindset. In this chapter, we familiarize ourselves with the practical strategies required to cultivate this mindset.

9.1. Understanding the Roots of Stoicism

When exploring the principles of Stoicism, its birthplace holds many keys to deeper comprehension. Ancient Greece and Rome were the nurturing grounds for this philosophy, brought into the world by the insightful minds of Zeno, Seneca, and Marcus Aurelius.

Let's briefly delve into the essence of what Stoicism preaches: life may not always be under our control, but our responses, attitudes, and actions always are. In a nutshell, it teaches acceptance of external events, and fostering an unshakeable inner peace.

The crucial element to remember about Stoicism is that it isn't a makeshift approach. Instead, it's an intensely personal philosophy, demanding a patient, disciplined adjustment to one's thoughts and manners, whilst undeniably promising lofty rewards.

9.2. The Four Cardinal Virtues of Stoicism

Stoicism is founded on four cardinal virtues that form the framework of a Stoic life. The mastery of these virtues is critical in developing a

Stoic mindset.

1. Wisdom: This involves understanding that our thoughts control our emotions, and hence cultivating logical, rational thinking. In business, wisdom aids in insightful decision-making, enabling the distinction between beneficial and detrimental ventures.

2. Courage: Not the physical courage of a warrior, but the mental courage to face adversity and endure through challenging times. It requires a steadfast dedication to one's principles, even when confronted by difficulties.

3. Temperance: This promotes the exercise of self-restraint and moderation. In entrepreneurship, temperance aids in maintaining emotional balance, making calculated risks, and avoiding reckless business decisions.

4. Justice: This virtue emphasises fair treatment of all. Practicing justice in your business interactions builds trust, encouraging stronger business relationships and fostering a positive reputation.

9.3. Adopting the Stoic Mindset: Practical Tactics

The key to developing a Stoic mindset lies in the adoption and consistent practice of specific tactics. Here, we share a few of the most impactful stoic practices for the entrepreneur.

Morning Meditation: Begin each day with a quiet reflection on your goals, responsibilities, and the potential challenges that might arise. Instead of fearing these obstacles, welcome them as opportunities to apply your Stoic virtues and grow. Use this time to remind yourself of the impermanence of success and failures.

Journaling: Maintain a daily journal, reflecting upon your experiences and emotions. Note your reactions to different situations, and analyze if your response was in line with the Stoic virtues. Self-scrutiny is the cornerstone of Stoic improvements.

Stoic Visualization: Visualize confronting situations that fire up your fears or anxieties. Imagine yourself responding to these situations with unfaltering Stoic calmness. This repeated visualization prepares you for real-life occurrences, enabling a truly Stoic response when actually confronted with the situation.

Negative Visualization: Consider the worst-case scenarios in your business. How would you react if your enterprise faced a severe crisis? The idea isn't to induce anxiety, but to comprehend that even the most challenging situations can be endured and ultimately used for growth through a Stoic approach.

The View from Above: This Stoic technique involves envisioning yourself from a third-person perspective or a bird's-eye view. It breeds the realization that your problems are tiny in the grand scheme of things, fostering a detached, objective view of your situations.

9.4. Practicing Discomfort

One of the more counterintuitive practices in Stoicism is the intentional induction of discomfort. Why? It's simple: to reduce the fear of adversity and increase resilience.

Start by introducing minor discomforts in your life – a cold shower, skipping a meal, or sleeping on the floor. As you get comfortable with discomfort, you'll find yourself less attached to comfort, and consequently, less disturbed by adversities.

Start small, practice consistency, and soon you will perceive a profound transformation. Unforeseen business crises would no longer unsettle you; instead, you would possess the unshakeable calm of a stoic entrepreneur.

9.5. Applying Stoicism in Business Decisions

A large part of entrepreneurship involves making crucial decisions that can make or break the business. The adopted Stoic mindset can be a beacon of guidance in this process.

A practical tool for entrepreneurial decision-making is the Stoic decision-making triangle, incorporating the cardinal virtues:

1. Wisdom: Evaluate all the possible truths and perspectives. Seek advice, consider potential consequences, and problem-solve logically.

2. Courage: Make bold decisions and stand by them. Courage is about making difficult decisions that others may shy away from.

3. Justice: Reflect on the impact of your decision on others. Aim for fairness and benefit for everyone involved.

4. Temperance: Exercise moderation and self-restraint. A tempered decision ensures balanced growth.

Developing a stoic mindset is not a one-time feat but a continuous journey of self-improvement. It's a commitment to oneself, a promise of calmer, rational, and, inevitably, a more successful entrepreneurial journey. Persist on this path, and you'll find that in every crisis hides an opportunity, and behind every adversity, you uncover a version of yourself stronger than before.

Chapter 10. The Stoic Entrepreneur's Toolkit: Navigating Business Uncertainty

There has always been a tight-laced kinship between Stoicism, an ancient philosophy steeped in practicality and pragmatism, and the chaotic yet rewarding world of entrepreneurship. This common thread arises from their shared emphasis on fortitude, resilience, and a relentless pursuit of ultimate objectives, irrespective of the prevailing circumstances. The Stoic Entrepreneur's Toolkit is an invaluable resource for entrepreneurs to navigate the choppy waters of business uncertainty.

10.1. Stoic Principles for Business Uncertainty

First, let's explore some of the critical Stoic principles that can light the path in the murky haze of business uncertainty.

Amor Fati – A Latin phrase that means 'love of fate,' this stoic philosophy promotes acceptance and even celebration of whatever comes our way. In entrepreneurial terms, it's about seeing every challenge or setback not as a hindrance, but rather as an opportunity to grow and improve.

Memento Mori – 'Remember you are mortal.' Stoics use this principle as a tool for humility and cherishing the moment. In business, we can apply it to help maintain balance and perspective, reminding ourselves that our time is limited, and failure is not the end of our story – it's just another chapter.

Ataraxia – Inner tranquillity, a state of serene calmness despite external circumstances. By practicing ataraxia, entrepreneurs can remain focused, composed, and clear-headed, even in a flustered business landscape.

10.2. The Toolkit: Practical Applications

Having defined the essential principles, let's delve into practical applications. How can these theories be translated into daily entrepreneurial tactics?

Mapping Out Stoic Decision Trees – Much like a chess player anticipates various moves and counter-moves, a stoic entrepreneur can chart out different scenarios for business decisions. This fosters ready responses and reduces uncertainty, ensuring calm during the stormiest business situations.

Stoic Journaling – Journaling promotes self-reflection, a core tenet of Stoicism. Entrepreneurs can journal challenges, their thoughts, reactions, and the steps taken. This reflective practice helps identify problematic patterns and fosters transformative improvements.

Practicing Negative Visualization – Picturing negative outcomes might seem counterproductive to the optimistic spirit of entrepreneurship. But Stoicism teaches us that by anticipating worst-case scenarios and planning for them, we can blunt their impact and respond more effectively.

10.3. The Power of Stoic Resilience

Resilience, the very essence of stoicism, behoves an entrepreneur to view every setback as a comeback in disguise. Embrace rejections, use them as fuel to ignite the engine of your efforts. As stoicism teaches, setbacks aren't obstacles on the path; they are the path.

10.4. Stoicism and Leadership

Stoic-driven leadership is about leading by example. The discipline of stoicism calls for a hands-on approach, instilling confidence and loyalty in your teams during chaos – particularly when business uncertainties hit hard.

10.5. Regular Introspection

Stoicism's introspective nature – the continuous analysis of our actions, reactions and the associated implications – provides a feedback loop for entrepreneurial growth and business strategy refinement. A process that proves invaluable during uncertain times.

10.6. Stoicism and Team Building

In team building, Stoicism's emphasis on understanding individual perspectives can help a leader empathise, enabling them to build stronger, more unified teams. This unity formulates a robust shield to withstand the buffets of business uncertainty.

10.7. Sustainability with Stoicism

Finally, the realm of business is filled with ups and downs. Stoicism – with its emphasis on resilience, acceptance, and humility – offers a sustainable approach for long-term success, providing entrepreneurs with tools to weather the storm of uncertainty and chart a steady course forward.

In conclusion, Stoic Entrepreneurship isn't about suppressing emotions or ignoring adversity. It's about acknowledging challenges, understanding their nature, and harnessing them as catalysts for growth – to build a stronger, better, more resilient entrepreneurial ethos. The process is tough, the journey long, but the rewards of Stoic

Entrepreneurship are compelling – they promise not just a successful entrepreneur but a wiser, balanced human being.

Chapter 11. Visions of Success: Stoicism as an Entrepreneurial Superpower

Plato depicted stoicism as an elevated state of consciousness, exclusive and transcendent. However, today's pragmatic stoicism simplifies it to one fundamental premise: While we cannot control all the events imposed upon us, we can control our response to them—a profound and transformative lens that, once applied to our entrepreneurial journey, alters everything.

11.1. Leveraging Stoic Teachings for Entrepreneurial Success

Stoicism, as a philosophy, encourages embracing life's complexities, accepting our inability to control all the bits and pieces that constitute the big picture. Yet, it simultaneously encourages us to harness our efforts on aspects that are within our control, such as the modality and essence of our perception.

As entrepreneurs, every business day is an amalgamation of complications and opportunities. How we translate these complexities sets us apart. Highly successful entrepreneurs view these "obstacles" as necessary steps to profound learning and growth.

Taking a broader look into perspective, all the colossal corporations today were once tiny startups. These tycoons witness an array of obstacles, but what sets them apart is how they perceived these challenges—not as an excuse for failure but as a pathway for growth.

11.2. Embracing Failure: The Stoic Way

Failure is an integral part of entrepreneurial ventures. Yet, it is widely viewed as a taboo that compels us to question the essence and credibility of the endeavor.

Stoic entrepreneurs differ by adopting the perspective that 'failure is not the opposite of success; it is part of it.' The wisdom lies in decoding the learning imbued in failures and leveraging them to refine business processes or entrepreneurial strategies.

Being flexible and adaptable in the face of failure and considering setbacks merely as redirecting paths paints the essence of stoic entrepreneurship. The true entrepreneurial superpower lies not within avoiding obstacles but harnessing the learnings produced by them.

11.3. Stoic Virtues: Implementing Modern Entrepreneurship

Historically, the stoic philosophy recognizes four key virtues: wisdom, courage, justice, and temperance. These virtues are not solely philosophical points of reflection, but translatable traits that can mold a successful entrepreneur.

To embody wisdom, for example, means an entrepreneur should always be in search of knowledge. This can be even more impactful as wisdom is not bound to classroom walls or limited to books but is present in everyday life's pursuits and challenges.

Courage in entrepreneurship is not merely about risk-taking, it is about making informed choices, standing by them, and believing in one's power to make a difference. It implies the courage to navigate uncharted territories, outperform competition, and innovate for a more sustainable and prosperous future.

Justice is another core pillar that implies doing what is right for the team, consumers, and society. Creating ethical solutions, respecting the environment, and ensuring corporate responsibility are virtues that all stoic entrepreneurs should hold dear.

Lastly, temperance can mean creating balanced approaches. Contingencies are inevitable in an entrepreneurial journey, yet leading with restraint and moderation enables an entrepreneur to navigate smoothly.

11.4. Applying Stoicism: Day To Day Operations

Once we grasp the virtues of stoicism, the next step is applying them in regular business activities. An essential part of this involves consistent contemplation.

Marcus Aurelius, a legendary stoic philosopher, regularly engaged in meditation. However, it's not the seated and silent meditation we tend to think of.

His meditation was an intellectual exercise where he revisited his actions, his challenges, and his efforts to align with stoic virtues. This meditative reflection can be ingrained into the entrepreneurial routine, where a daily manifestation of actions, responses, and dynamics can be assessed against the pillars of courage, wisdom, justice, and temperance.

11.5. Stoicism and Leadership

An entrepreneur is a leader, and successful leaders inspire and motivate. Stoicism, with its intrinsic emphasis on virtues like justice and fairness, can be leveraged to develop credible leadership.

Transparency, openness, and consistent communication exhibit courage and authenticity, further fostering trust and engagement within the team, paving the way for a unified and high-performing squad with a shared vision.

Also, embracing the virtue of temperance, leaders can commit to open mindedness, and weaving diversity and inclusivity into the core fabric of their venture. Not only does this provide a firm foundation for the organization, but it also paves the way for a rich culture promoting creativity and innovation.

11.6. Epilogue: The Entrepreneurial Journey

Entrepreneurship is not a rigid pathway; it fluctuates, vibrates, and demands us to do the same. With stoic philosophy acting as an adhesive, entrepreneurs can align their actions and reactions, ensuring they remain grounded amidst a whirlwind of challenges and opportunities.

In the grand tapestry of entrepreneurship, obstacles thread the path to achievement. As we navigate this complex journey, we find that every misstep, every stumble, underpins remarkable opportunities for growth and advancement.

Stoicism isn't merely a philosophical adornment; it's an entrepreneurial superpower—a key to resilience, optimism, and indomitable success in our endeavors.

www.ingramcontent.com/pod-product-compliance
Lightning Source LLC
Chambersburg PA
CBHW071034260726
48661CB00007B/3024